Sunrise

Grayce Levan

Presentation by *BookLeaf Publishing*

Web: www.bookleafpub.com

E-mail: info@bookleafpub.com

ISBN: 9789357448611

First edition 2022

DEDICATION

To the person who inspired some of the happiest poems in this book, you know who you are. Thank you. No matter what the future holds for us, you gave me some of the happiest memories I've had in a long time. I hope that will continue for a long time, but if, god forbid, it doesn't I hope you'll remember me as fondly as I'll remember you. But if you don't and you decide to throw this book out, just make sure not to litter. ;)

ACKNOWLEDGEMENT

Thank you to my three best friends for always supporting me and inspiring me to do better. You helped me grow as a person to get to the point I'm at now, and I hope to continue to grow with all of you for years to come. Special thanks to the girl who helped me figure out the title.

Halfway

I haven't known you long.
I've got no right to write a poem or song.
But the truth is I care more than I care to admit.
And I feel like I'm a hypocrite,
Because I try so hard to pretend
That I don't panic all the time thinking it's the
end.

You've already proven me wrong so many
times.
You make excuses for all of my crimes.
And I just feel like somehow you set me free,
Like you somehow make a better version of me.

So I guess I believe in love,
Even if I never find it again.
I guess there are signs from above,
That I shouldn't get my worth from the opinions
of men.
And I don't know what the future holds for us,
But that just might be okay.
You've proven there are people who deserve my
trust,
And maybe that gets me halfway.

Platonic

I don't like that you own my heart,
But I can pretend
That it didn't break apart,
Since you just want to be my friend.
Maybe it's not ideal,
But I can pretend
That my friendship is real,
If it means that it's not the end.

Would it be weird if I said I loved you,
Just in a platonic way?
I mean that's really not true,
But I don't know what else to say.
Cause I'm kind of struggling
With masking my affection.
And it's kind of troubling
How much I feel there's a connection.
So would it be weird if I said I loved you?
Just in a platonic way?
Even though it's not true,
Be that as it may
I don't know what else to do,
Would it be weird if I said I loved you?

You know, actually, it might be true,

Since it occurred to me
I'll love you any way you want me to,
No matter what I want us to be.
I just want to see you smile,
Even if I'm not the reason why.
As long as you're happy for a while,
I'll be pacified.

Is it weird if I say I love you?
Just in a platonic way?
Because that really is true,
No matter what I say.
I just want you to be happy,
And I want that as a friend.
Because you mean everything to me,
And that's never going to end.
So is it weird if I say I love you?
Just in a platonic way?
Since that really is true,
And with that I'm okay.
I know what I want to do.
So is it weird if I say I love you?

Recycling

We recycle
Because the illusion of choice
Is much more bearable than the reality
Of helplessness.
We want so desperately
To believe that the brief,
Bright moment in which we're alive
Means something.
And corporations comply
Because anything less
Would lead to anarchy,
Or worse, democracy.

Meaning in the Gray

When did the notion of seizing the day
Become something uneasy to attain?
We work so hard now, and what do we gain?
But days upon days of numb, endless gray?
My mind is at work, but my heart may stray,
Longing for something that's not quite so plain.
Wishing for something it cannot obtain.
But, as always, I have nothing to say.
Since it's people who give life a meaning,
I need not grieve for those who are waking.
Look close enough to see their hearts gleaming.
Shimmering, even when they are aching.
Beauty is nothing to hearts convening.
People themselves are all that's breathtaking.

Sunrise

You don't know it,
But when I say you're special, it's freeing.
I don't take those words lightly.
They come from every fiber of my being.

Of course, I would never lie,
About the way I feel for you,
But you might think it's just because,
I've felt that for other people too.

But what I haven't told you is that
I've never wanted to befriend
Anyone else I've felt this for
For me, you've broken every trend.

You're the first to keep my attention,
And I don't mean this in a bad way.
Because no matter what happens between us,
I care about you enough to stay.

And I think that must be the crucial difference
That I've always been looking for,
Between a favorite person and actual love.
And every day I like you even more.

This isn't like my usual hot red passion,
But it's not the peaceful golden glow I'm told
normal love should be.
This is something different, something in
between,
Like the color of the sunrise high above the sea.

I don't mean to be off-putting,
It's true that my love may be different from the
rest.
But I don't ask for anything in exchange,
Since you make me the version of myself that is
best.

For once, my love isn't something selfish,
Something designed to only benefit me.
Because I would take on all the pain in the
world,
Just to make you happy.

And I would be anything for you that you
wanted,
Which is something I haven't really felt before.
It's always been about protecting myself,
But you, you I'd do anything for.

So I don't need anything in return,

I'm not going to pine for you as I've done in the past.
Because I don't need anything to appreciate you.
Compared to others, you're such a contrast.

And I know you don't know how amazing you are,
But someday I'm going to convince you.
I'll keep reminding you that you're great,
Until you believe it too.

Another Universe

Sometimes, I wish I could tell you
Of all the thoughts swirling in my mind.
But don't worry, I won't let them break through
Out of the place I have them confined.

But maybe in another universe
I wouldn't have to pretend my feelings were
reversed.
I'd tell you how insatiably jealous I am of her
Instead of letting resentment stir.

Maybe I'd tell you how much I really care
Instead of hiding how fond I am of you.
And making sure you weren't aware
Of everything I know to be true.

I'd stand tall, I'd take a chance,
Unafraid of it not ending in romance.
The truth is I do like you that way,
Even if it sounds a little cliché.

Maybe in another life,
I'd let go of all of my fears.
Someday maybe I'd be your wife,
And we'd be happy throughout the years.

Such pretty thoughts I have about you and me,
And how perfect all of it would be.
Of course, I wouldn't admit it now and here,
But not only because of my fear.

You seem happy with her,
So I'll leave it be.
Since I couldn't make you happier,
And I don't believe anyone would ever choose
me.

Still now and again it feels nice to dream
Of a love that gives off a warm golden gleam.
So I'll indulge my heart for just five more
minutes,
Until my brain reminds it of my limits.

And I'll smile, happy to just be your friend,
Since this way is safer,
And less likely to end.
I just hope the other me knows what she has to
savor.

The Thing About Dystopias

Do you remember when we were young?
The tire swing and the tree from which it
swung?
We'd read books like The Hunger Games,
And thought a dystopian society to be so
strange!
Divergent made a dystopia sound fun,
We all believed we'd be the chosen one.
We wished to live in such an exciting world,
With twists and turns where danger unfurled!

Later we grew up and we learned,
That we lived in a dystopia - just like we'd
yearned.
Only this dystopian world wasn't quite fun,
There was no one to save us - no chosen one.
Two handsome boys didn't create your love
triangle.
You didn't have all that drama to wrangle.
And the villains in the story,
Weren't brave - they only wanted their glory.

There were no good intentions,
Their green paper god was the only thing they
cared to mention.
Everywhere you looked, the men at the top,
Their hands dripped crimson red nonstop.
There were enough bodies to fill a ravine,
From all the victims crushed in their money
machine.
And yet even with my heart heavy with grief,
I still hope that someday there will be relief.

And I hope that someday you won't know my
name;
That such a notion of violence is an
unreasonable claim!
They say those who forget are bound to repeat it,
We're called to remember - but I don't believe it.
"Another victim with no justice, remember their
name,"
But no martyr wants that to be their reason for
fame.
I hope you forget all the names piling up, not
just because they become statistics,
But because you can't even imagine a mad man's
characteristics.

Of course when I was a child, neither could I,
I'd watch horrors play out without even batting
an eye.

And you see that's the thing about living in a
dystopia,
We can't see how savage it is due to our own
metathesiophobia.
And yet I have hope for future generations,
Our youth will revive our corrupted home
nation.
There will be a world in which every human can
fit.
I just won't be alive when the time comes to see
it.

Do you remember when we were young?
The tire swing and the tree from which it
swung?
If so, my sweet child, you're far too early.
But know, there will come a day humans are
once again worthy.
However, if you can't recall a time with such
lawful lawlessness,
You're lucky, dear reader, but proceed with
cautiousness.
And if a leader starts screaming they can make
you great,
You must turn your back on their heart filled
with hate.

Splitting

They always talked about splitting,
How I see things as all good or all bad.
And I always thought it was fitting,
Because it's the way I always had.

But now it seems like I'm splitting,
Into multiple versions of me.
And I'm having a hard time admitting
That I do know why that would be.

On one side jealousy's burning my skin,
Gagging with envy and distain.
This feels like a competition to win,
You're something I'd cheat to attain.

But the other side is much softer,
Soothing me into a hush.
It doesn't want me to stop her,
Or let you know of my crush

I've always been boiling with rage,
Setting fire without a care.
Even though anger backs me into a cage,
Wanting to be tranquil is rare.

Part of me thinks I could do better,
That I could treat you as you deserve.
But based on all my past letters,
I'd do better to stay in reserve.

For once there are things that I wouldn't do,
I've got boundaries in place.
And for that I'll give credit to you,
That I'm surrendering with grace.

So maybe I let my mind run away,
And dream of a killing spree.
But overall I think I'm going to be okay,
Taking deep breaths and counting to three.

I'm okay with you being with her,
Because for you she seems to be good.
So it doesn't matter who you'd prefer,
Because she makes you happy in ways I never
could.

Favorite Person

Freedom when love lifts me high upon its wings,
As I picture your sweet caress and the happiness
it brings.
Vacant would my heart be without your
attention.
Oh, my love for you is beyond comprehension.
Radiant is the fire in your soul,
I feel that with you, I'm finally whole.
Transfixed by your smile, caught in your gaze,
Enchanting my life in marvelous ways.

Perhaps you're just passing by me tonight,
Even so, the sight of you fills me with delight.
Revive me from my heart's endless sleep,
So that I may be yours to keep.
Once upon a time, I fell for you,
Now it's yours to decide if you want me too.

Failure cingulates around my heartstrings.
Answer me! Do you care how much it stings?
Voids swallow me whole as reprehension,
Obligated to strand me in suspension.
Ruthless is your heart made of coal,
Insistent that you always have complete control.

Though for you, I was only a phase.
Elegies promise to be all for me that stays.

Prideful are you, born out of spite.
Endless darkness promises I'll never feel alright.
Rapid tears coat my cheeks as I weep,
Since you tossed me away like I was cheap.
Occupied by the solemn silence, I knew,
Never will you leave me, even though we're
through.

Why Aren't You Afraid?

My flame flickers and dances on your tongue.
You're the tree I grow my ivy around.
You're a planet flying too close to my sun,
Cuz when I think back on everything now,
Suddenly my life becomes opaque.
Maybe I've been sleeping
When you made me feel like I was awake,
Sneaking into every breath you're breathing.

I stand here on the edge of everything I've
known,
In a crowded room but all alone,
Deceitful truths about myself causing deafening
silence.
The girl inside me is just too defiant,
And I try to ignore her like the plague,
But she's just the monster I made.
You wouldn't be here if you only knew,
But it'll also hurt me to hurt you.
I don't wanna see that look in your eye wishing
you hadn't stayed.
So why aren't you afraid?

And I burn everything I touch to ash,
Grow my ivy tighter and tighter.
Protecting you from any and all backlash,
Everything except my whims and desire.
I wrap myself so close to you,
Wilfully ignorant of you getting shaky.
They say you're suffocating but we don't think
that it's true,
Cuz I look like such an innocent lady.

All my demons have grey eyes,
Like ash from my blaze.
They'll say it's brilliant to agonise,
Being devoured by my golden-pink rays.
When I look to the future,
Just what do I want?
A chance to be your suitor?
Or just another romant?

My demons were once like you but historically,
I find some bullshit reason to flee,
When they have nothing left to give me.
And I watch the light in their eyes die when I
leave them in the debris.
And I don't feel remorse cuz I warned them well
to a degree,
They've always known there was something
wrong with me.

I stand here on the edge of everything I've
known,
In a crowded room but all alone,
Deceitful truths about myself causing deafening
silence.
The girl inside me is just too defiant,
And I try to ignore her like the plague,
But she's just the monster I made.
You wouldn't be here if you only knew,
But it'll also hurt me to hurt you.
I don't wanna see that look in your eye wishing
you hadn't stayed.
So why aren't you afraid?

Resistance

When you're standing on the edge of a cliff,
Sometimes it's easier to let yourself fall.
Especially when you know that you'll live,
Since the water at the bottom saves us all.

But you scratch, and you claw, at the rocks,
Just trying to hold yourself up.
And you break, and you bleed, you can't talk,
Without screams to interrupt.

You resist every inch of the way.
And you pray, and you beg, and you plead,
That you won't fall today.
Even though at the bottom is everything you
need.

Because if you fall you lose all control,
But no one can resist falling in love.
It feels wrong, but you know it's right in your
soul,
So you let go, and descend from above.

Crazy

I haven't known you forever,
But that's how long we'll be together.
You're my entire world, moon and stars.
You make me forget about my scars.
I put you up, up on a pedestal.
And my friends are all sceptical,
So I'll cut them out of my life,
Because I would kill to be your wife.

I would die for you,
I'd commit murder right now if you asked me to.
What? You didn't text me back?
Well, I'll destroy myself over that,
Or I'll go talk to your manager,
convince him you're an amateur,
And get you fired so you'll have more time for
me.
Do you still believe I'm not crazy?

The truth is I'm terrified you just don't believe
All of the things that I know about me.
And I'm scared of what you'll do
When you wake up and realize they're true.
I'm crazy, and not just about you.

Closure

They've always said
That your entire life can be changed
By a fleeting act of kindness from a stranger. I
never understood what they meant,
Until now. There's a calm about this situation,
The thought of him leaving me like this
would've left me in the wreckage
Of my life before.
This feels deliberate, purposeful, divine even.
I should be upset that he isn't staying
In my life, but maybe he wasn't meant to.
Maybe in ten years I won't remember
His face, or even his name.
But I will remember that
He gave me hope in a time
That I needed it most.
I'll remember that he taught me
There are still good people in the world
And what I'm looking for IS out there.
And that's enough.

Okay, maybe I am a little hurt,
Which sours the lesson a little.
I just wish I knew what I did wrong.
Even though it's probably better

If I don't know. Everything just feels different.
I was thinking that this
Was supposed to give me hope
That I would find someone,
But maybe it did the opposite.
Still, I guess I believe in love,
Even if I never find it again.

I'm Sorry

I don't really have thoughts anymore,
Other than the ones of you.
I know it's not like it's been before,
But to me everything is still new.

It's exhausting biting my tongue all the time.
Is it manipulative to hold myself back?
Or is it a victimless crime?
My heart constantly repeats the same
soundtrack,
One that I would never speak aloud.
Because it would probably scare you away.
And nevertheless I'm far too proud.
So this is where those thoughts will stay.

That's why I'm writing this down I presume,
So it doesn't come out in screams.
But I'm going to acknowledge the elephant in
the room,
The things I say only in my dreams:

I love you.
I love you.
I love you.
I love you.

I'm sorry.
I love you.

Fears

Everyone always tells me how great I am.
How great a friend,
How great a worker,
How great it is to see me happy.
But the truth is I don't know if I'll ever believe
any of it.
So many people say they love me,
But I don't think I deserve love.
I constantly regret my place in their lives,
Because I believe I'm fundamentally
unloveable.
And it's true I'm doing so much better
Than I was before,
But I don't know if I'll ever be able
To love myself like I want to.
And I know I'll never be able to love myself
The way I love others.
And if it's to much to ask of myself,
How could I ever ask that of anyone else?
I pretend like I don't think that anymore,
Fake it til you make it I guess.
But in my heart I still believe I'm going to die
alone.
And I don't know if that's ever going to change.

Your Jacket

I've never liked sitting in the rain,
But I'd probably do anything with you.
Although I continue to feel less and less sane,
Reading so much into everything you do.

Your jacket was warm, but you made me feel
warmer inside.
Maybe it was just the flush on my cheeks I was
trying so hard to suppress.
I probably couldn't even though I tried.
Mostly though I think the night was a success.

It's surprising how such little moments can seem
To go on for evermore.
Even if they seem like they could have just been
a dream.
Living in our hearts folded into a little drawer.

And I know to you it probably wasn't that big a
deal,
But even if we end up growing apart,
I'll always remember how that moment made
me feel.
I'll save the memory for a rainy day in my heart.

I Hate Me Not You

I thought you were so great,
But now my love's turned into hate.
Maybe you don't even have a heart at all,
To leave me alone staring at the wall.

I guess I'll never understand.
I guess it's just the way I am.
How can someone hurt another like this?
And leave them in a dark and cold abyss.
I think you're a horrible person.
Maybe you were never even worth it.
But ever since the moment that I knew,
I hate me not you.

You just lied right to my face.
If you'd told the truth I would've gone with
grace.
How hard would it have been to say,
That you didn't intend to stay?
You didn't want to be my friend,
You just wanted our conversation to end.
So why keep talking to me like it's fine,
When you knew our intentions didn't align?

I guess I'll never understand

I guess it's just the way I am
How can someone hurt another like this
And leave them in a dark and cold abyss
I think you're a horrible person
Maybe you were never even worth it
But ever since the moment that I knew
I hate me not you

And the worst part of it all
Is I know I'd forgive you the second that you call
But you won't

Real Things

The difference between a favorite person
And real love is that you'd do
Anything to get a favorite person
To like you, but if you're in love
With them, you'd do anything
To make them happy.
Even if it hurts you.
Even if it's not with you.
Even if their happiness isn't possible
If you are in their life.
That's the difference I've always been looking
for
And I feel better, wiser for having
Even known you in the first place.

Downfall

I had a dream last night,
Our love was something in sight.
It was possible.
We were possible.
I could picture you and me,
It was something that could be.
I felt like I could fly.
I could see you and I.

If I'm gonna have a downfall it's gonna be you.
I need to focus on what I have to do.
I don't wanna fall into your trap,
Can't afford to let you hold me back.
Falling for you is my downfall.
You're my fatal flaw,
Most destruction that you ever saw.
If I'm gonna make a mistake,
To cause a lot of heartache,
If I have a downfall,
Baby, you're my downfall.

I have a dream tonight.
It's to set my sight
On someone else.
Is that possible?

I can still picture you and me,
Like it's something that could really be.
I can still see it all,
But you won't catch me if I fall.

Falling for you is my downfall.
You're my fatal flaw,
Most destruction that you ever saw.
If I'm gonna make a mistake,
To cause a lot of heartache,
If I have a downfall,
Baby, you're my downfall.

This Moment

I don't mean for this to sound sappy,
But even if we grow apart I'll remember I was
happy.
This moment in time when you were part of my
world,
When all the colors around me swirled.
That's what I'm always going to remember,
Every September, November, December.
And I would miss you of course,
But I don't think you'd have a reason to worry or
remorse.
Because I think you've helped me grow,
To a point I'm not dependant on you, although,
I still savor every second I get with you,
Saving them up for if my fears come true.

What Now?

Now, now that you've finished reading this,
I almost wish to pretend,
To be ignorant with bliss,
About the words that I've penned.

Can we just act like it's not about you?
To save me a little shame?
That it's just something I wrote, not something
true?
Even if we both know it all the same?